Angels and Archangels

for Children
and Those Who Love Them

*Love!
Anne Mason Taylor*

Anne Mason Taylor

Archangel Michael Slays the Devil by Reni, 1575–1642.

First Printing

Copyright © 2018 by Anne Mason Taylor, L.L.C.

All rights reserved. No part of this book may be reproduced or transmitted in any form or by any means, electronically or mechanical, including photocopying, recording, or by any information storage and retrieval system, without the written permission of the author, Anne Mason Taylor.

Anne Mason Taylor, Author, Editor, and Publisher

Published by Anne Mason Taylor, L.L.C.

ISBN: 978-0-692-18451-6

Printed in U.S.A.

Angel icon by Freepik from flaticon.com

To obtain a copy or many copies of

Angels and Archangels for Children and Those Who Love Them,

Please contact:

Anne Mason Taylor, L.L.C.

AngelsandArchangelsAMT@gmail.com

(919) 725-6001

Table of Contents

Quote from Hebrews 7

Dedication 9

Preface 11

Introduction 15

Angel Rainbow 19

Angel Alphabet 21

Letters and Lessons 23

How Angels Work 74

George Washington's Vision of an Angel 76

Angels Answer Prayer 81

Photograph of an Angel 84

Angel Blessings 87

"Be ye not forgetful to entertain strangers;
For thereby some have entertained angels unawares."

Hebrews 12:3

Archangel Michael (Protects)   Archangel Raphael (Heals)   Tobias   Archangel Gabriel (Announces)

Dedication

This book is dedicated to
All Good and Holy Angels in Heaven and on Earth,
And to all those who believe in,
And work with God's Angels.

Angels inspire Joan of Arc (Jeanne d'Arc) to save France.

Preface

Angels are in every religion on planet earth.

In Judaism, the Old Testament teaches us how Archangel Michael rescued the three Hebrew boys from Nebuchadnezzar's fiery furnace when they refused to deny their faith in God.

Archangel Michael stopped Abraham from sacrificing his only son, Isaac, when Abraham showed God that the Lord was first in his life, second to no one and no thing. God was pleased, sent the angel to protect the boy, and God made Abraham the Father of all nations.

In Christianity, the New Testament records how Archangel Gabriel announced to Mary that if she was willing, God needed her to give birth to Jesus, the incarnate Word of God and true Son of the Lord. Mary, pure of heart, mind, body and soul loved and trusted God. "Behold the handmaiden (servant) of the Lord. Thus, be it unto me." The angel of the Lord announced the birth of Jesus Christ to the good shepherds who came to worship the newborn babe. A sword pierced through Mary's own heart, also, as she watched her son suffer on the cross. And she became Mother of all in Heaven and on earth.

Archangel Michael appeared to the young peasant girl of Orleans, Jeanne d'Arc (Joan of Arc), and guided her to meet with the French King to give her soldiers, weapons and horses to lead an Army to save France. With the King's supplies, she led the army and saved France from the British. Later, beginning in 1776, France sent soldiers and weapons to America's colonial army and helped win the American War of Independence from Great Britain.

During the Korean War, American and South Korean soldiers were saved when Archangel Michael slew Communist North Korean mercenaries during a blinding snowstorm. The communists were slain by a sword, and American U.S. Marine soldiers wrote home about the tall, handsome, blonde being who suddenly appeared to help them named, "Michael."

The official Russian newspaper, Pravda, in the late 20th century, reported that a group of Russian cosmonauts all witnessed an amazing site when they looked outside the windows of their spacecraft. Angels, as large as jumbo jets, smiling mysteriously as if they knew a deep and important secret, were flying alongside the airship.

And during World War II, air fighter pilots reported miracles with angels. Captain Bill Overstreet, U.S. Army Air Corps, P51 Mustang fighter pilot Ace, saw angels "around his cockpit escorting his plane" in the spring of 1944, when he took off from his airbase in Leiston, England. "At first, I thought it was battle fatigue, but angels on both sides of my cockpit guided me and stayed right with me for quite a while until I got to 30,000 feet over Germany."

Minutes later, Captain Overstreet chased a German Nazi Messerschmitt 109 under the Eiffel Tower in Paris, which was under German Nazi occupation. The Nazis aimed their tanks, German planes and other ground and air weapons at Bill's plane to destroy him. Miraculously, Bill shot down the Nazi Messerschmitt as he flew out from under the Eiffel Tower, and Bill made it safely back to base. Until this miraculous flight, the French had given up and the Nazis had fully taken over Paris. Allied orders were for no Allied planes to enter Paris, but Bill fought on. His flight that shot down the Nazi plane under the Eiffel Tower gave the French people, who had stayed in constant prayer, new hope that the Allies were coming to help save France. As a result, French Freedom Fighters known as the French Underground, who had earlier given up hope, jumped back on their feet. One man with faith and angels, Captain Bill Overstreet; one plane, the Berlin Express; and one selfless flight to save others helped to free an entire nation, France, and eventually all Europe.

When you work with God and the Angels, and believe, miracles happen. And when you pray to God to send to you his angels for help, they always come.

Angels are in every country throughout the history of mankind. They are throughout Judaism, Christianity, Buddhism, Muslim folklore, Zoroastrianism and every other religion on planet earth.

Angels arc the blessings of God to us below, but they may not interfere with mankind's free will. They may only respond to our prayers and calls.

God will answer every prayer as you pray and call to the angels, provided you follow God's laws:

>First, your prayer must be for a good and pure purpose;
>Second, your prayer must fulfill God's will for you and others; and
>Third, you may not ask for undue harm to yourself or others.

>Believe and have Faith.
>Call to the angels.
>They will always come.

Introduction

When a beam of light strikes a crystal prism, it divides into seven(7) colors of a rainbow: blue, golden yellow, rose pink, white, green, purple, and violet.

Each of these seven color vibrations of light stands for each of seven great Archangels of God. An archangel is an angel of highest rank. Each of the seven Archangels archs a divine principle of God as their color to us on earth.

Each archangel is masculine and directs their specific divine mission principle for God to us on earth when we pray to them in the name of God. Each archangel also has a feminine archangel, known as an Archeia (Greek for feminine archangel) who as an equal partner, works with her Archangel to serve mankind and arc their specific principle of God to us on earth below.

God created the angels before He made mankind so the angels would be in Heaven and on earth to help us. But angels are not allowed to interfere with mankind's free will. They must be asked to help us. The word angel means messenger of God.

The seven Archangels and their feminine Archeai work most strongly within their specific colors and missions for God to help us on earth. They are: Archangel Michael and Archeia Faith (sapphire blue), Archangel Jophiel and Archeia Christine (golden yellow), Archangel Chamuel and Archeia Charity (rose pink), Archangel Gabriel and Archeia Hope (pure white), Archangel Raphael and The Blessed Mother Mary who is also an Archeia (emerald green), Archangel Uriel and Archeia Aurora (purple) and Archangel Zadkiel and Archeia Holy Amethyst (violet).

In ancient writings, they correspond to and send their Godly energies most strongly on certain days of the week. Archangel Michael and Faith shine most strongly on Tuesday. Archangel Jophiel and Christine shine most strongly on Sunday. Archangel Chamuel and Charity shine most strongly on Monday. Archangel Gabriel and Hope shine most strongly on Friday. Archangel Raphael and Mary shine most strongly on Wednesday. Archangel Uriel and Aurora shine most strongly on Thursday. And Archangel Zadkiel and Amethyst shine most strongly on Saturday.

    Each Archangel and Archeia team arc their specific Godly principle.

    Archangel Michael and Faith bring Will of God, Power of God, Faith in God, and angelic protection of God. They come in sapphire blue. Archangel Michael is famous for his mighty sword of blue flame.

    Archangel Jophiel and Christine bring wisdom, illumination, and Divine Intelligence from God's infinite wisdom in the golden glow to us from the mind of Christ.

    Rose pink is arched to us by Archangel Chamuel and Charity. The word Charity, in ancient Hebrew, also means love. Love is the strongest power force on planet earth. When love from your heart is intensified most strongly, the pink color grows deeper and deeper until, with the greatest love, it turns the color of blueish-red, a deep ruby red of the blood of Christ, the world's ultimate love of giving oneself for others.

    Pure white is alchemically a perfect presence and balance of all of God's colors and divine principles with which He created the rainbow and each of us. It is the pure light and pure motive of The Holy Spirit, or in ancient Hebrew, The Holy Spirot of God. With their white light, Archangel Gabriel and Hope bring us God purity and hope. Archangel Gabriel came to the Virgin Mary who was pure in thought, word, and deed, and asked her, on behalf of God, if she would agree to become the Mother of God Incarnate, or in human form as Jesus the Christ. Mary answered, "As it be the Will of God, it shall be done…" Hope, purity and communication are the blessings increased within us by Archangel Gabriel and Hope.

Healing, truth, and science are the gifts most strengthened within us by Archangel Raphael and the Blessed Mother Mary with emerald green. When you need healing, pray to Archangel Raphael and Mary to bring their emerald green healing angels into your body, mind, soul and spirit. Archangel Raphael brought healing to Tobit, also known as Tobias in the book of Tobit, to heal Tobias on his wedding night when Archangel Raphael instructed Tobias to eat the gall of a fish. It worked!

Archangel Uriel and Aurora come on the deep purple and gold beams to bring us Peace of God. When Saint Francis met a friend along the path, he first raised his right hand with a smile and greeted them with the single word, "Peace." For he knew nothing of permanent accomplishment can be built without first having a spirit of peace. A peaceful spirit can build. A chaos energy can only destroy. We wish to build only goodness with a peaceful spirit within ourselves.

The violet color of the rainbow is arched by Archangel Zadkiel and Holy Amethyst. Violet hues bring freedom, mercy, and forgiveness. When we forgive others, we cut ourselves free from the record, memory and energies of the difficulty. We not only give others the blessing of mercy, but we also by becoming free of the problem, receive a blessing for ourselves. William Shakespeare knew this as he taught us in his play, *The Merchant of Venice* with Portia's speech that,

> "Mercy is twice blessed. It blesses him who gives,
> And him that receives."

Make your life happy. Pray to the angels who arc the colors of God's rainbow to magnify and increase God's blessings to you. They will come when you pray to bring you love, mercy, forgiveness, hope, safety, power, truth, wisdom, peace, healing, joy and the spirit of knowing that with his angels, you are in the heart of God.

Angel Rainbow

The Archangels and Archeia Who Arc Specific Blessings

When the Lord created the world, God created seven days in the week, seven notes to a chord, seven major centers of glands and organs in the human body, seven colors in the rainbow, and seven senior Archangels and female Archangels, known as Archeia. Each of the seven pair of Archangels and Archeia arc a basic principle of God to earth within their special color vibration.

Sapphire Blue. Archangel Michael and Archeia Faith bring power of God, protection, safety, strength, and God's Will. Archangel Michael is "Captain of the Hosts of the Lord." He is head of all God's Archangels and Angels. Pray to Archangel Michael and Archeia Faith to protect you.

Emerald Green. Archangel Raphael and the Blessed Mother Mary bring healing from God, truth, science, and abundance. Pray to them to heal you and to bring abundance.

Purple. Archangel Uriel and Archeia Aurora bring peace, contentment, and harmonious relationships. Pray to them to resolve conflicts and bring peace in your life.

Violet. Archangel Zadkiel and Archeia Amethyst bring mercy, freedom, forgiveness, and help us change from sin and problems into holiness and blessings. Pray to them for forgiveness.

Rose Pink. Archangel Chamuel and Archeia Charity bring love, beauty, and kindness. Pray to them to teach you loving kindness, creativity, and to find your true love.

Golden Yellow. Archangel Jophiel and Archeia Christine bring wisdom, Divine Intelligence, and understanding. Pray to them to bring Divine knowledge, wisdom, and the Light of Christ.

Pure White. Archangel Gabriel and Archeia Hope bring purity, hope, joy, and discipline that results in victory. Pray to them for hope, purity, communication skills, and a joyful spirit.

Angel Alphabet

Aa Bb Cc Dd Ee

Ff Gg Hh Ii Jj Kk

Ll Mm Nn Oo Pp

Qq Rr Ss Tt Uu

Vv Ww Xx Yy Zz

A is for Angels,
They fly through the sky,
They bring me God's love,
And are always nearby.

Melozzo da Forlí, Italian, 1438–1494

B is for Bright,
As their Light shines from God.
There's no problem I'll have
That the Angels can't solve!

C is Call to the angels to help you.
They'll come.
They are powerful, wise,
Loving, and fun!

D is at Daybreak,
They kiss me awake.
I'm secure in their strong arms of love
For my sake.

E is their Energy,
Spirit, and Light.
Magical, Holy,
And full of Delight!

F is for Faith,
And the strength that it brings.
When I focus on angels,
I feel I have wings.

G is for Grace.
I am calm and Divine.
Angels pour God's love
Through my body and mind.

H is for Heaven,
And Heavenly ways.
My thoughts and my footsteps
Are sound and worth praise.

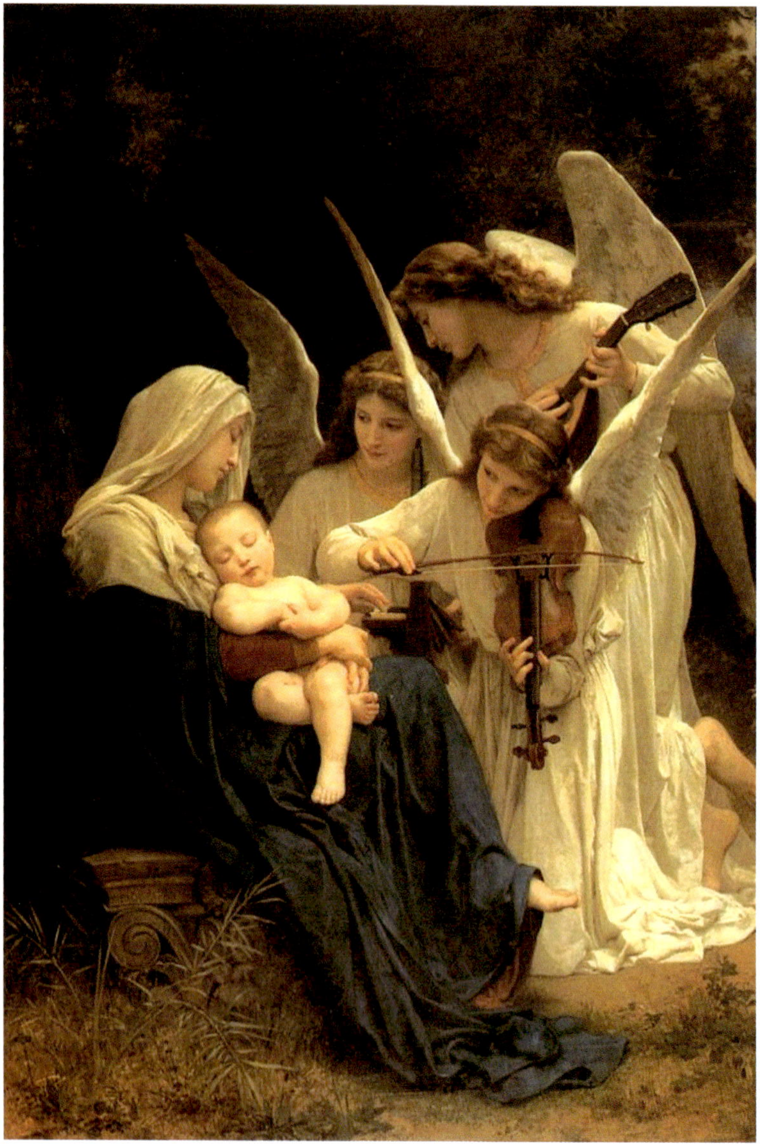

I means, "I hear angels".
Their golden harps play.
They guide me, protect me,
In all kinds of ways.

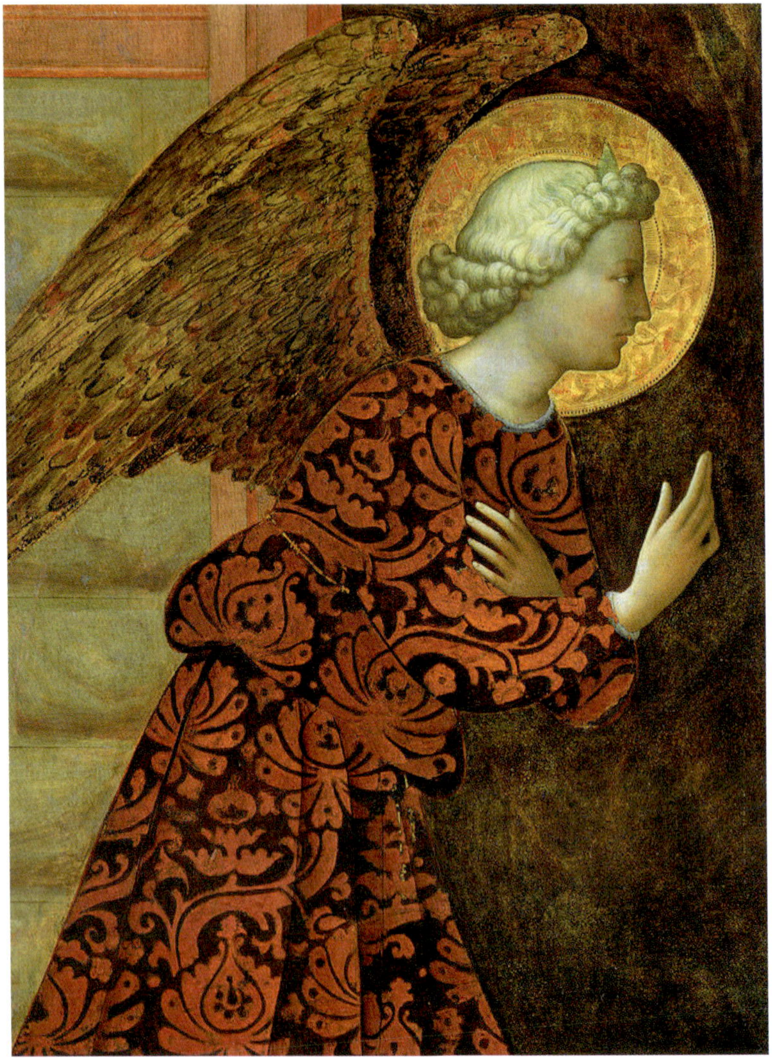

J is for Jolly,
And Strong, and Secure.
I sense all these angels protect me,
For sure!

Archangel Gabriel by Tiffany

K is for Kindness and Truth
Are my Guide.
My life is so happy,
My heart does take stride.

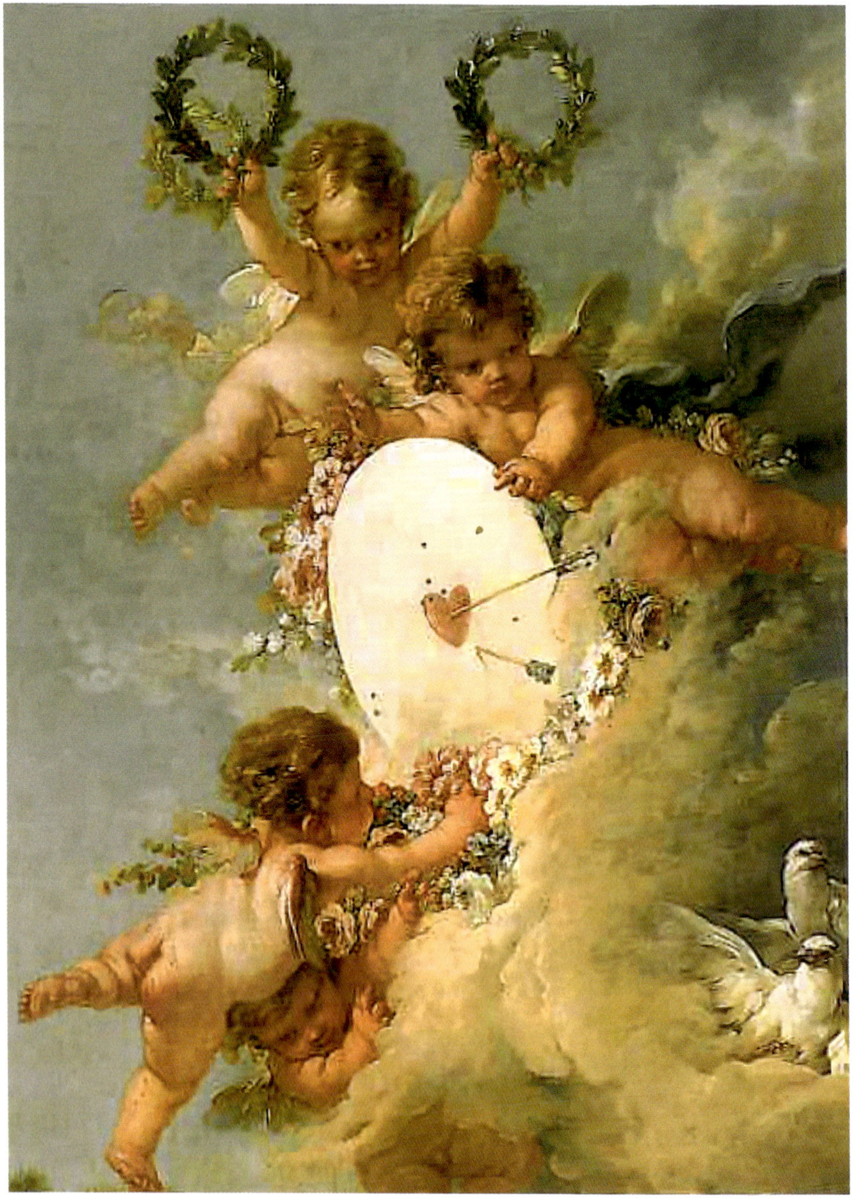

L is for Love will Abide.
It is True.
Angels bring love,
And they're always "true blue".

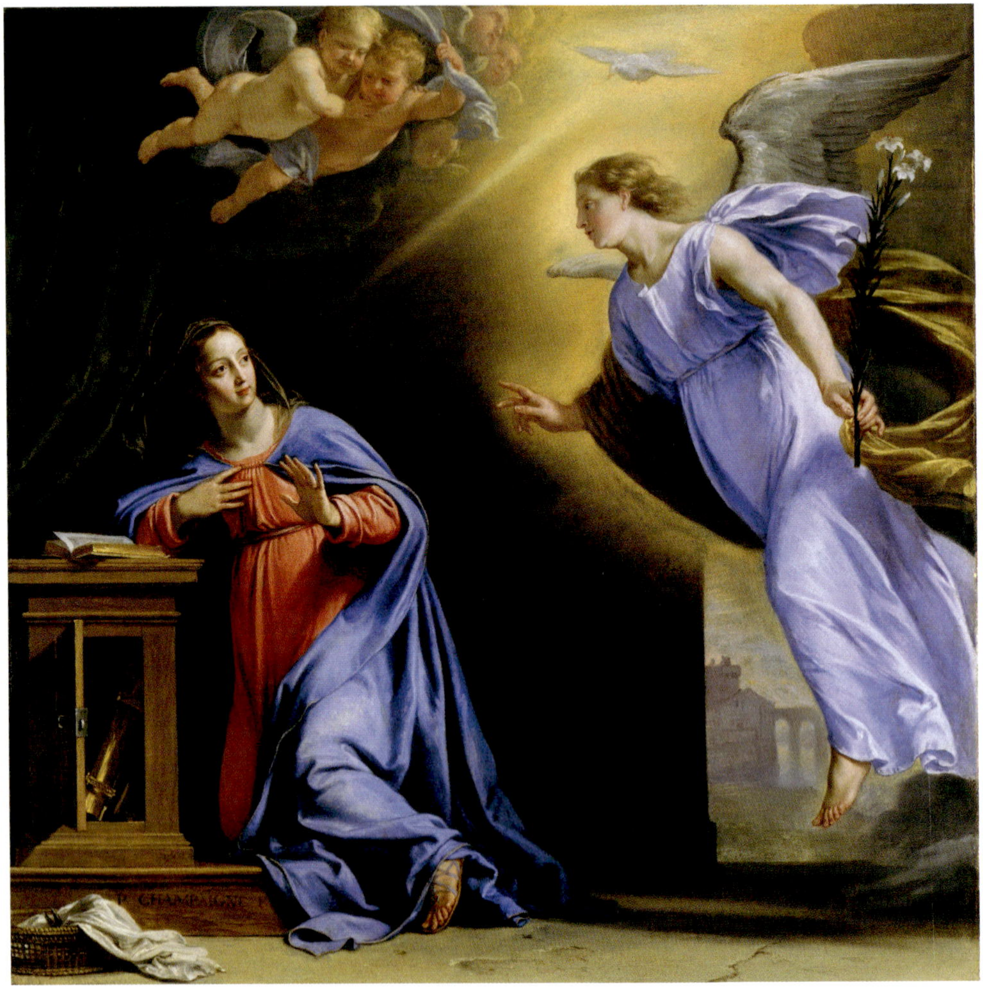

M is for Mary,
Christ's Mom, knew this well.
The Archangel Gabriel
To Mary, did tell.

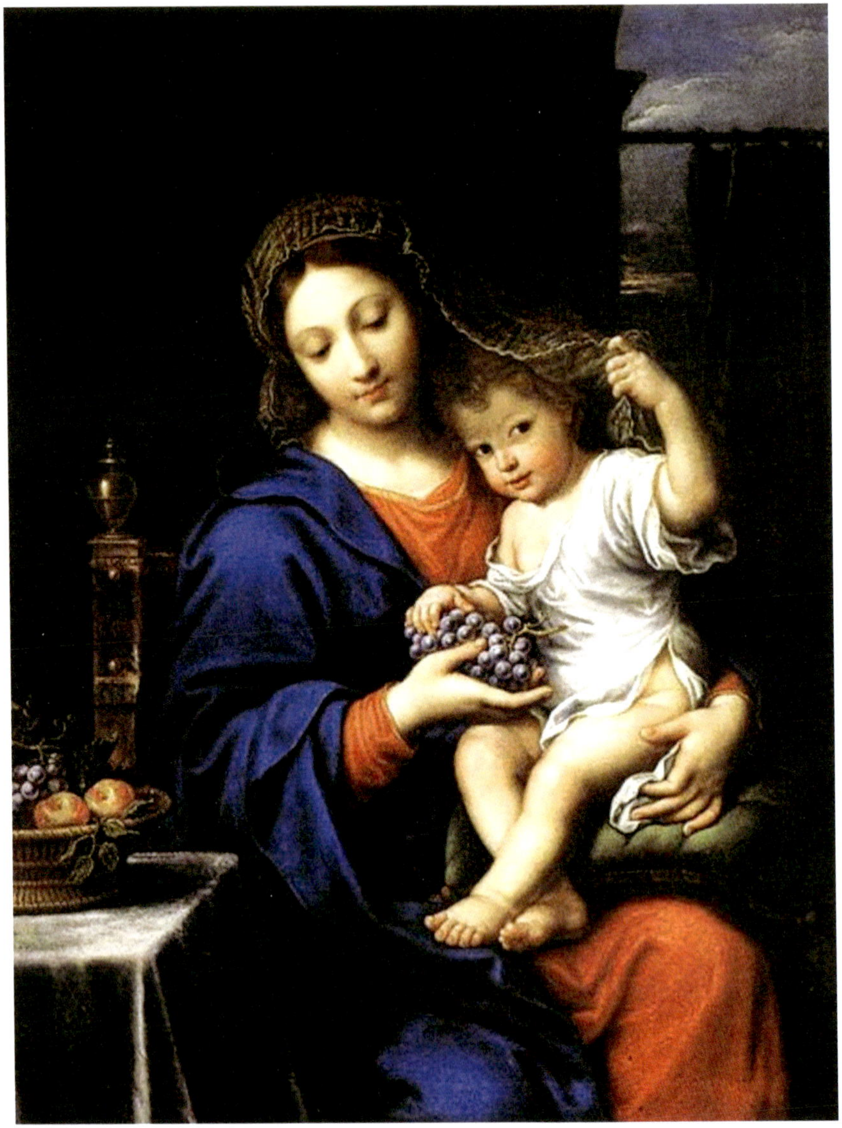

N is for Never Doubt that
Christ came!
The Angels announced Him,
And called Him by name.

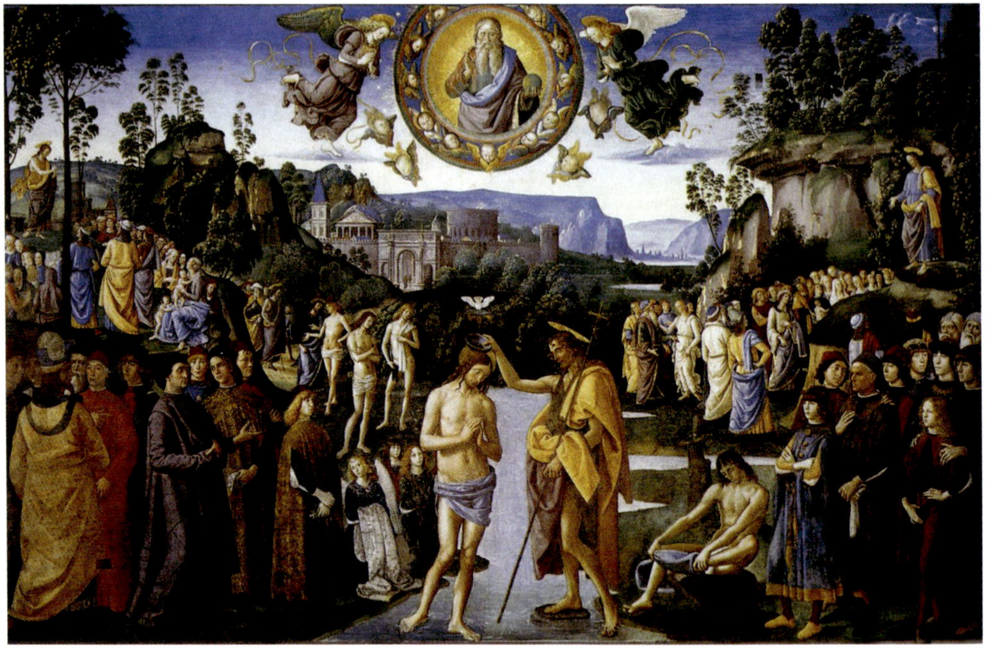

O is Open each Heart
To that Love.
Emmanuel came,
With a Heavenly Dove.

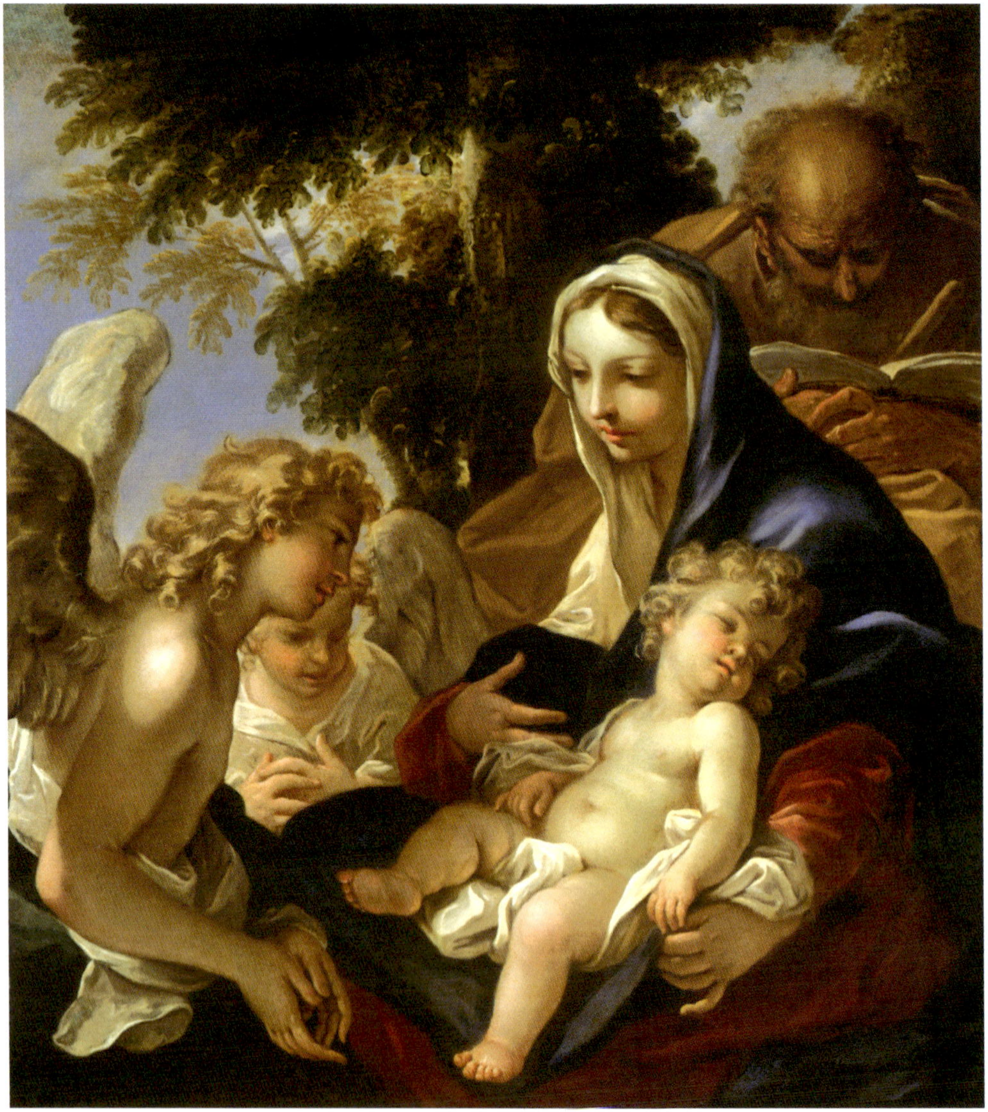

P is the Peace
Jesus brings to my heart.
He'll always be with me,
And never depart.

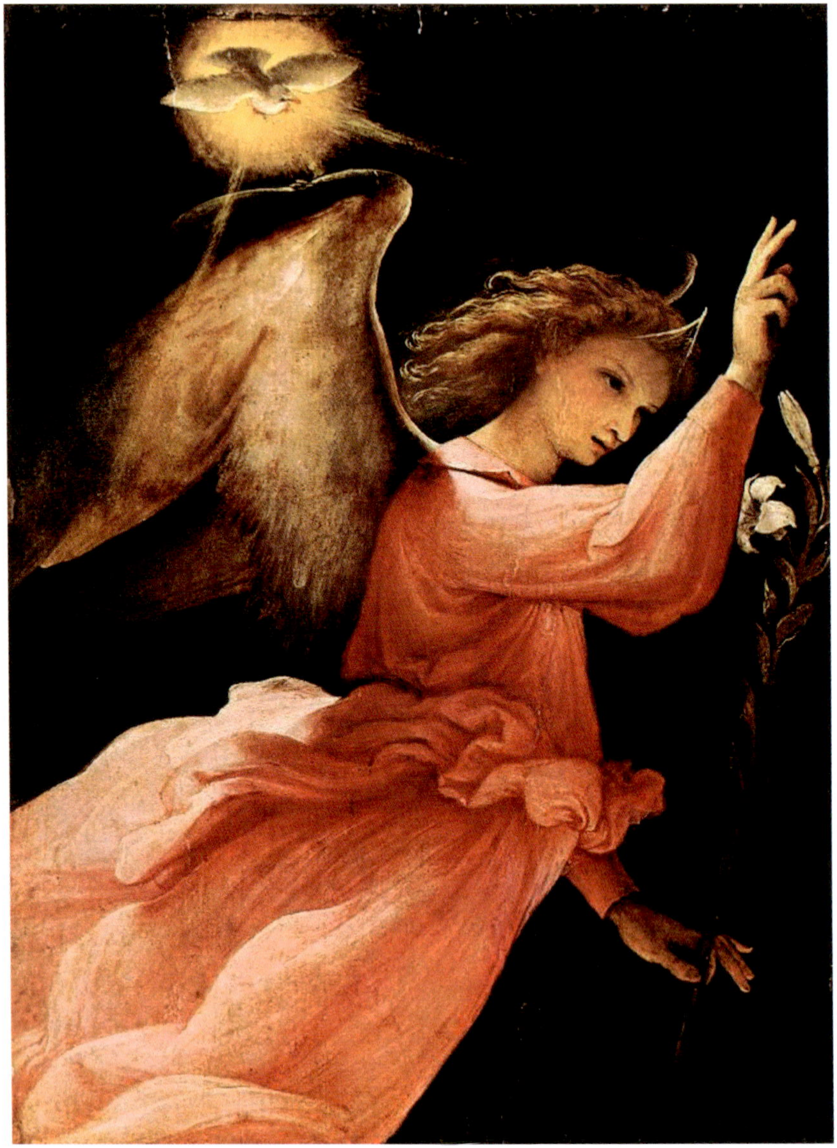

Q is for Quests
I can conquer and solve.
When I work with the angels,
My life is resolved.

Gustave Doré, 1832–1883

R is Reach for the Stars
And Believe!
When I pray and I listen,
I'll always achieve.

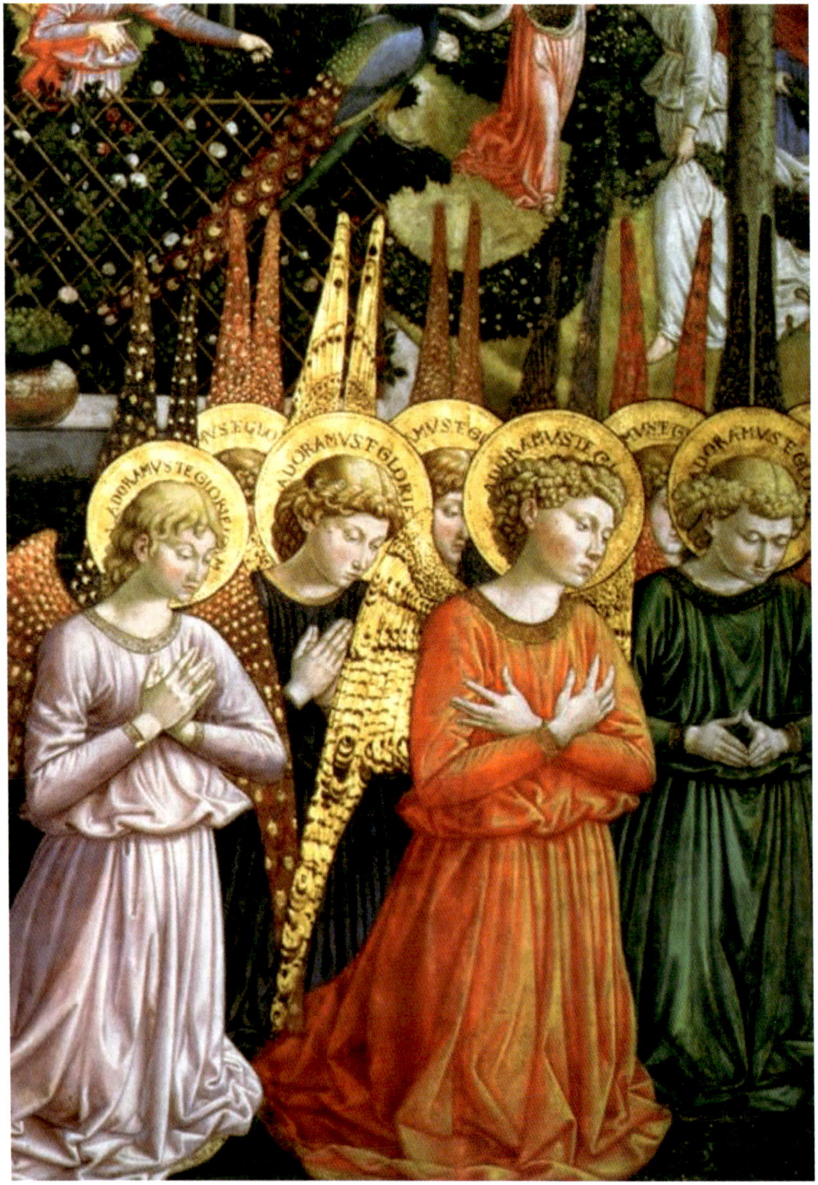

S is for Stretch
My mind and my muscles.
Achieve all my goals,
Avoid all the tussles.

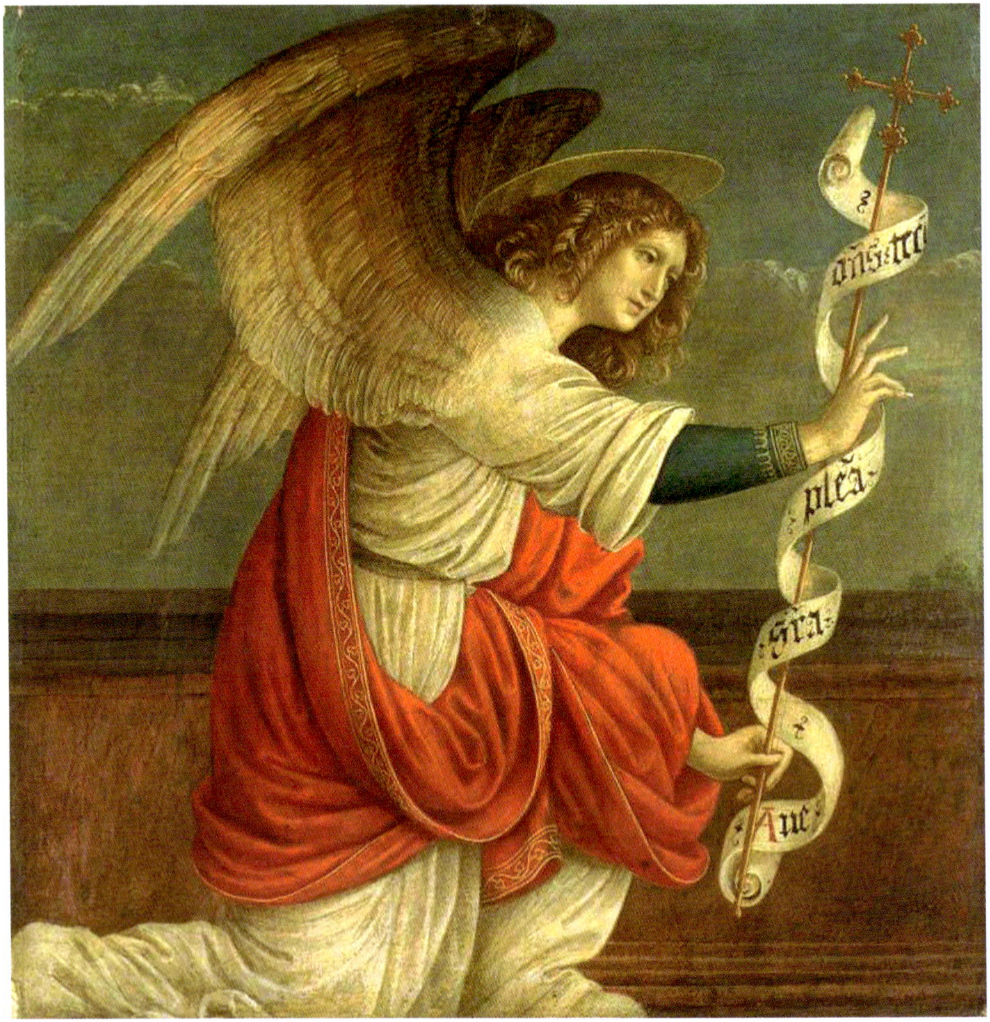

T is for Trusting
My conscience within.
Do good. Have faith.
Keep my chin up, and grin.

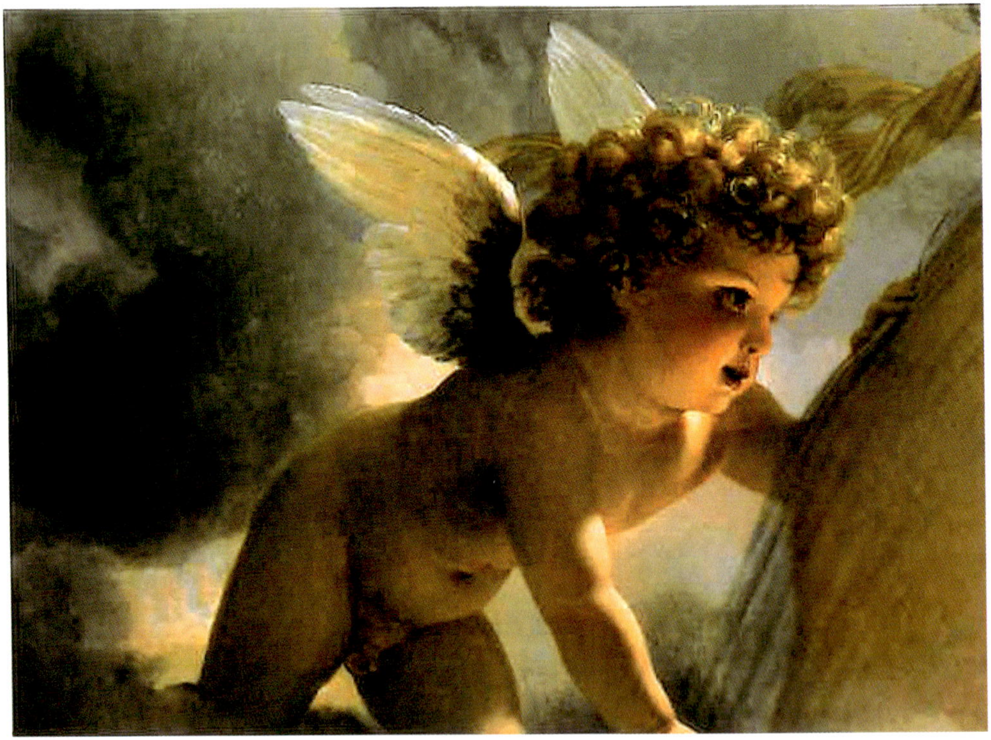

U is Unanimous!
All do agree.
I'm the happiest spirit.
I get it. I see!

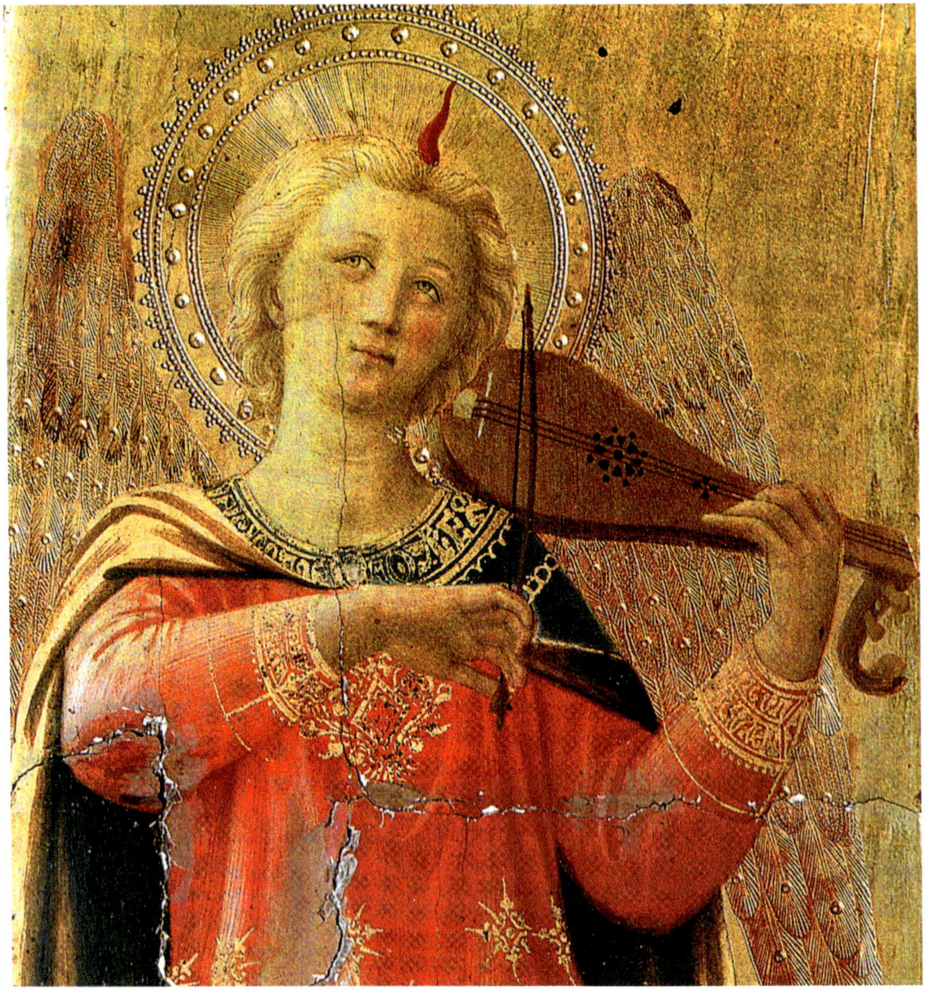

V is for Victory
For me in this life.
Rest, pray, and work,
And I'll win against strife.

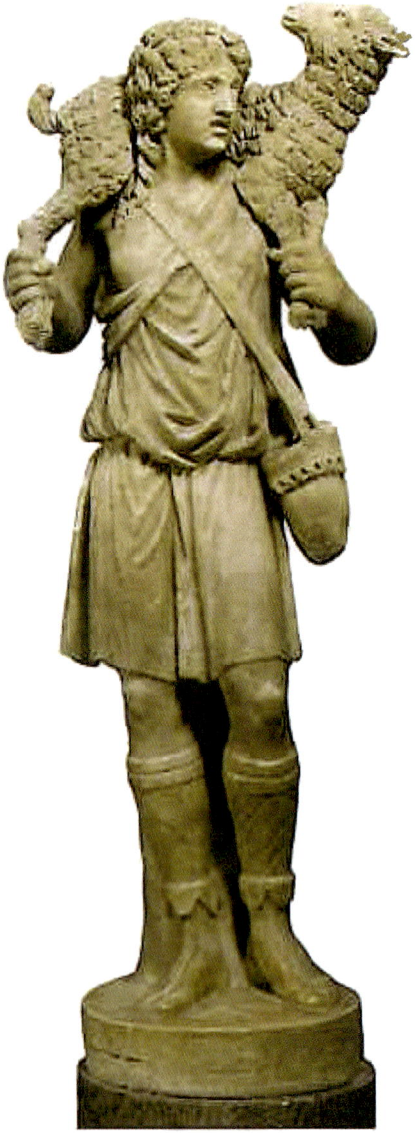

W is to win,
I must play a fair game.
Be honest. Work hard.
Help the lonely and lame.

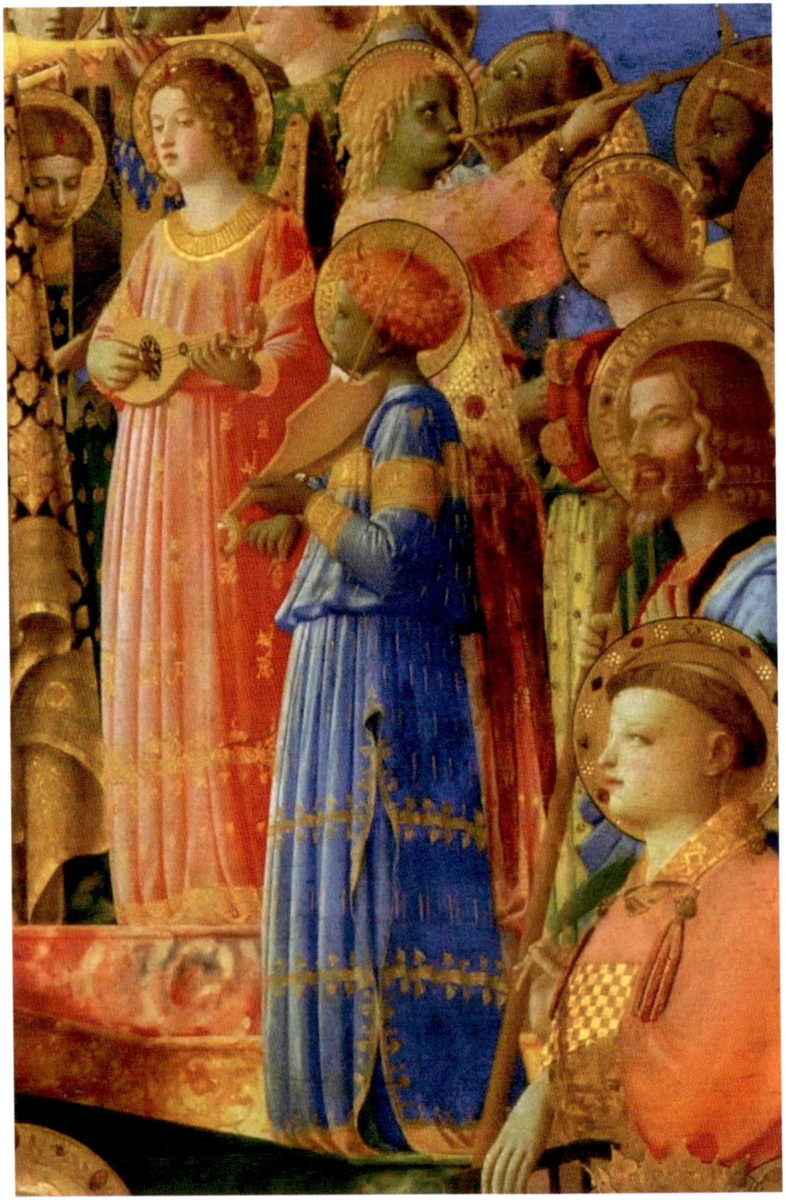

X is for Xylophones,
Trumpets, and Harps.
Angels play music
That strengthens our hearts.

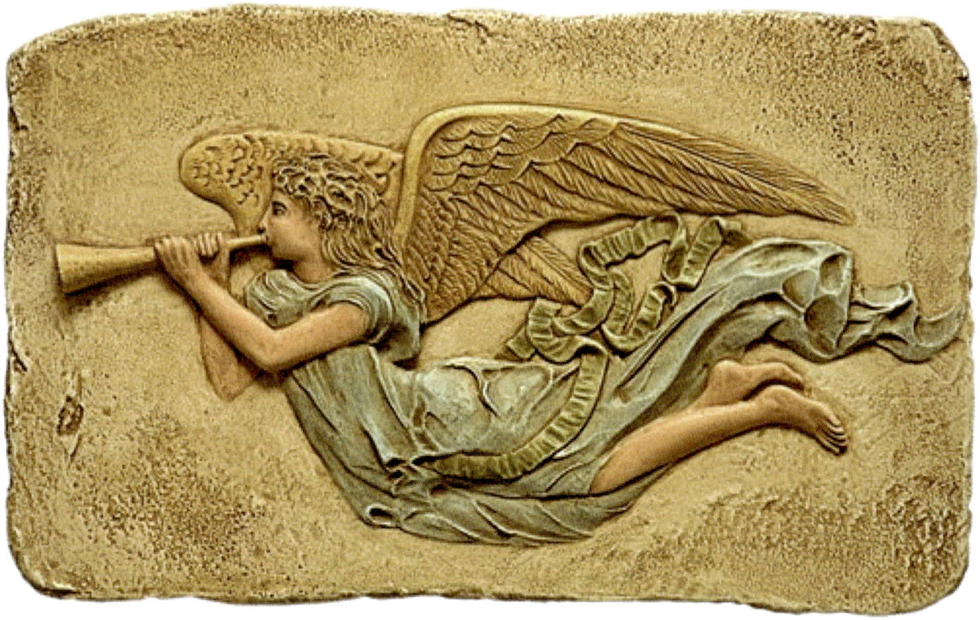

Y is my Youth
Is for learning to be,
The very best me
For the Angels to see!

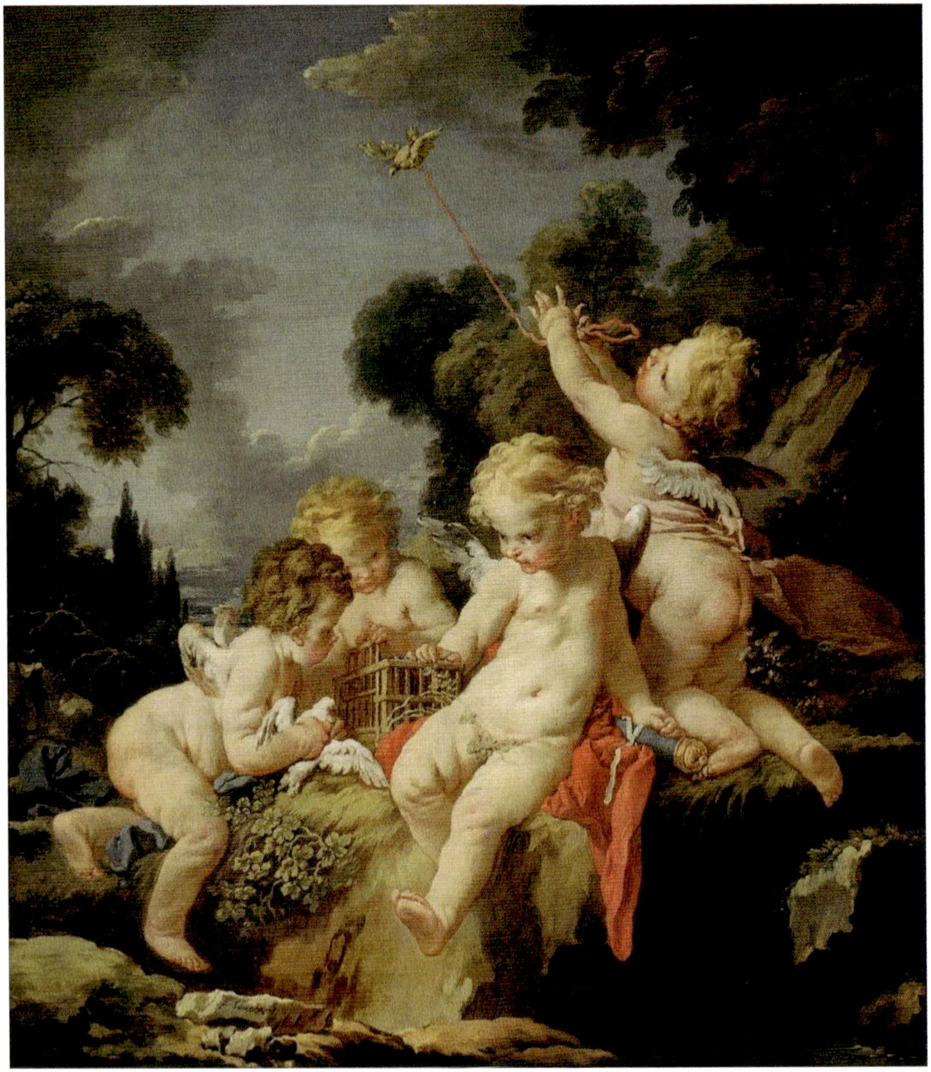

Z is for Zebras,
Dogs, and birds, too.
All of God's creatures
Who purely love you!

How Angels Work

Angels do arc
The light from the sun,
That's been sent from the Father
Since earth was begun.

'Tis the love of the Spirit,
The Light of the Christ,
That lives in each person
That gives us all Life.

The angels bring forth
God's Heavenly Love,
In service to people
From Heaven Above.

They serve God and man,
If only we pray,
For them to help us,
Throughout every day.

They will not interfere
With the freewill of man.
But will answer your prayer
With a wise, helping hand.

If you just make a call,
"Dear Angels, please come!
Please guide me, Protect me,
I'm God's daughter, God's son."

So keep faith in God,
Know your angels are near.
Ask them always to help you
Each day of the year.

"In the name of Jesus the Christ,
Please Come, Archangel Michael, Come!
Help me! Help me! Help me!
Amen."

Washington's Vision

    A Divine Angel of God appeared to General George Washington when he and his men were fighting for freedom from Great Britain during the American Revolutionary War.

    On Christmas night at Valley Forge in 1776, our Army was literally freezing, starving, and praying for help. About to quit, our Commanding General, who loved his soldiers and trusted God, prayed constantly for guidance.

    An angel appeared and showed General Washington why he must continue the battle for human freedom that would change forever the destiny of mankind. The United States of America was founded, consecrated and established by God to give mankind an environment of liberty within which to be free to make individual choices. Only with freedom of choice can man develop wisdom and learn to be as God. We must choose right over wrong and good over evil.

    General Washington's report of the appearance of the angel was verified, documented, and published as true since 1880 and is reprinted here.

WASHINGTON'S VISION OF AMERICA'S TRIALS

Originally published by Wesley Bradshaw
Copied from a reprint in the National Tribune
Volume 4, Number 12, December 1880
And further reprinted within
The Official Documents of the United States of America's
Bicentennial on the U.S. Constitution and
The Congressional Record Of the United States House of Representatives,
Washington, D.C.

The last time I ever saw Anthony Sherman was on the fourth of July, 1859, in Independence Square. He was then ninety-nine years old, and becoming very feeble. But though so old, his dimming eyes rekindled as he gazed upon Independence Hall, which he came to visit once more.

"Let us go into the hall," he said. "I want to tell you of an incident of Washington's life – one which no one alive knows of except myself; and, if you live you will before long, see it verified.

"From the opening of the Revolution we experienced all phases of fortune, now good and now ill, one time victorious, and another conquered. The darkest period we had, I think, was when Washington, after several reverses, retreated to Valley Forge, where he resolved to pass the winter of 1776.

"Ah! I have often seen the tears coursing down our dear commander's care-worn cheeks, as he would be conversing with a confidential officer about the condition of his poor soldiers. You have doubtless heard the story of Washington's going into the thicket to pray. Well, it was not only true, but he used often to pray in secret for aid and comfort from God, the interposition of whose Divine Providence brought us safely through the darkest days of tribulation.

"One day, I remember it well, the chilly winds whistled through the leafless trees, though the sky was cloudless and the sun shone brightly, he remained in his quarters nearly all the afternoon alone. When he came out I noticed that his face was a shade paler than usual, and there seemed to be something on his mind of more than ordinary importance.

"Returning just after dusk, he dispatched an orderly to the officer I mention who was presently in attendance. After a preliminary conversation of about half an hour,

Washington, gazing upon his companion with that strange look of dignity which he alone could command, said to the latter:

"I do not know whether it is owing to the anxiety of my mind, or what, but this afternoon as I was sitting at this table engaged in preparing a dispatch, something seemed to disturb me. Looking up, I beheld standing opposite me a singularly beautiful female. So astonished was I, for I had given strict orders not to be disturbed that it was some moments before I found language to inquire into the cause of her presence.

"A second, a third, and even a fourth time did I repeat my question, but received no answer from my mysterious visitor except a slight raising of her eyes. By this time I felt strange sensations spreading through me. I would have risen, but the riveted gaze of the being before me rendered volition impossible. I assayed once more to address her, but my tongue had become useless. Even thought itself had become paralyzed. A new influence, mysterious, potent, irresistible, took possession of me. All I could do was to gaze steadily, vacantly at my unknown visitant.

"Gradually the surrounding atmosphere seemed as though becoming filled with sensations, and luminous. Everything about me seemed to rarify – the mysterious visitor herself becoming more airy and yet more distinct to my sight than before. I now began to feel as one dying, or rather to experience the sensations which I have sometimes imagined accompany dissolution. I did not think, I did not reason, I did not move; all were alike impossible. I was only conscious of gazing fixedly, vacantly at my companion.

"Presently I heard a voice saying, "Son of the Republic, look and learn," while at the same time my visitor extended her arm eastwardly. I now beheld a heavy white vapor at some distance rising fold upon fold. This, gradually dissipated, and I looked upon a strange scene. Before me lay spread out in one vast plain all the countries of the world – Europe, Asia, Africa, and America. I saw rolling and tossing between Europe and America the billows of the Atlantic, and between Asia and America lay the Pacific.

"Son of the Republic," said the same mysterious voice as before, "look and learn." At that moment I beheld a dark, shadowy being, like an angel, standing, or rather floating in mid-air, between Europe and America. Dipping water out of the ocean in the hollow of each hand, he sprinkled some upon America with his right hand, while with his left hand he cast some on Europe.

"Immediately a cloud raised from these countries, and joined in mid-ocean. For a while it remained stationary, and then moved slowly westward, until it enveloped America in its murky folds. Sharp flashes of lightning gleamed through it at intervals, and I heard the smothered groans and cries of the American people. A second time the angel dipped water from the ocean, and sprinkled it out as before. The dark cloud was then drawn back to the ocean, in whose heaving billows it sank from view.

"A third time I heard the mysterious voice saying, "Son of the Republic, look and learn." I cast my eyes upon America and beheld villages and towns and cities springing up one after another until the whole land from the Atlantic to the Pacific was dotted with them. Again, I heard the mysterious voice say, "son of the Republic, the end of the century cometh, look and learn."

"At this the dark shadowy angel turned his face southward, and from Africa I saw an ill-omened spectre approach our land. It flitted slowly over every town and city of the latter. The inhabitants presently set themselves in battle array against each other.

"As I continued looking I saw a bright angel, on whose brow rested a crown of light, on which was traced the word "Union", bearing the American flag which he placed between the divided nation, and said, "Remember ye are brethren."

"Instantly, the inhabitants, casting from their weapons, became friends once more, and united around the National Standard.

"And again I heard the mysterious voice saying, "Son of the Republic, look and learn." At this the dark, shadowy angel placed a trumpet to his mouth, and blew three distinct blasts; and taking water from the ocean, he sprinkled it upon Europe, Asia and Africa.

"Then my eyes beheld a fearful scene: from each of these countries arose thick, black clouds that were soon joined into one. And throughout this mass there gleamed a dark red light by which I saw hordes of armed men, who, moving with the cloud, marched by land and sailed by sea to America, which country was enveloped in the volume of the cloud.

"And I dimly saw these vast armies devastate the whole country and burn the villages, towns, and cities that I beheld springing up. As my ears listened to the thundering of the cannon, clashing of swords, and the shouts and cries of millions in mortal combat, I heard again the mysterious voice saying, "Son of the Republic, look and learn." When the voice had ceased, the dark shadowy angel placed his trumpet once more to his mouth, and blew a long and fearful blast.

"Instantly a light as of a thousand suns shone down from above me, and pierced and broke into fragments the dark cloud which enveloped America. At the same moment the angel upon whose head still shone the word Union, and who bore our national flag in one hand and a sword in the other, descended from the heavens attended by legions of white spirits. These joined the inhabitants of America, who I perceived were well-nigh overcome, but who immediately taking courage again, closed up their broken ranks and renewed the battle.

"Again, amid the fearful noise of the conflict, I heard the mysterious voice saying, "Son of the Republic, look and learn." As the voice ceased, the shadowy angel for the last time dipped water from the ocean and sprinkled it upon America. Instantly the dark cloud rolled back, together with the armies it had brought, leaving the inhabitants of the land victorious.

"Then once more I beheld the villages, towns, and cities springing up where I had seen them before, while the bright angel, planting the azure standard he had brought in the midst of them, cried with a loud voice: "While the stars remain, and the heavens send down dew upon the earth, so long shall the Union last." And taking from his brow the crown on which blazoned the word "Union," he placed it upon the Standard while the people, kneeling down, said, "Amen."

"The scene instantly began to fade and dissolve, and I at last saw nothing but the rising, curling vapor I at first beheld. This also disappearing, I found myself once more gazing upon the mysterious visitor, who, in the same voice I had heard before, said, "Son of the Republic, what you have seen is thus interpreted:

"Three great perils will come upon the Republic. The most fearful is the third passing which the whole world united shall not prevail against her. Let every child of the Republic learn to live for his God, his land and Union."

"With these words the vision vanished, and I started from my seat and felt that I had seen a vision wherein had been shown to me the birth, progress, and destiny of the United States."

"Such, my friends," concluded the venerable narrator, "were the words I heard from Washington's own lips, and America will do well to profit by them."

Washington Crossing the Delaware, Emanuel Leutze, 1816–1868

Angels Answer Prayer

God sends angels to answer prayers.

The angel appeared to General George Washington in answer to his prayers to God to guide him. When he saw the angel's vision of America's future, George Washington had new hope, new courage, and knew just what to do!

That night, Christmas, December 25, 1776, he and his men crossed the Delaware River into New Jersey in the bitter freezing ice and snow. They captured Trenton, New Jersey, their first victory in the American Revolutionary War.

With this great news, Dr. Benjamin Franklin in Paris, France, convinced King Louis XVI and his wife, Queen Marie Antoinette, to help the Colonial Army defeat England. The King agreed and sent soldiers, ships, supplies and weapons to help us.

With the help of France, America won the American Revolutionary War and America grew to become great, just as the angel had shown.

Doctor Benjamin Franklin by Joseph Siffred Duplessis

General George Washington by Gilbert Stuart

Photograph of an Angel

At the time Jesus was born, evil King Herod ordered his men to kill every Jewish baby boy in Jerusalem. The King knew the ancient scriptures taught that at that certain time, based on Divine astrology, a baby boy would be born destined to be "King" and Herod did not want his power, money or position threatened. Herod believed the child had been born, but did not know who or where the baby was.

At the same time, Archangel Gabriel appeared as a vision/dream to Joseph and instructed Joseph to quickly take Mary and their new-born son, baby Jesus, and "flee!", which means, "run away, fast!" Joseph did not know about Herod's murder decree, but Joseph trusted the Archangel and believed in God who had sent him.

The Holy Family quickly left Jerusalem in the dark before dawn and with one faithful donkey, began walking swiftly toward Egypt, where they would be safe. After a few days, as they went forward through the desert sands, they found a huge rock and stopped to rest and pray. Their faith flowed from their hearts as they rested and prayed at this spot.

Hundreds of years later, men built a church upon the rock. But this area in Egypt's Holy land has, for thousands of years, constantly suffered war, battle, and death. Soldiers fight each other over whose religion is right and which nation should own what land. At this writing, the battles continue.

The Jews fight the Christians. The Christians fight the Arabs. And everyone fights the Moslems. This holy church stands strongly and silently in the midst of all the fighting. And soldiers from every land and religion lay down their weapons at the entrance doors, and come inside to pray for peace. Each one knows the church is also a temple, a mosque, and the home of God, no matter what faith you use to pray to God.

In the 1980s, a group of religious seekers, pilgrims, traveled from the United States of America to visit the church/temple/mosque in the village outside Xitung, Egypt. The American group of visitors entered the prayerful place and the women and men silently walked to the front altar where – for thousands of years – the soldiers have been praying to God for peace to end the wars.

As the group was at the altar, one lady who stood praying suddenly felt a strong sense of love and peace cascade from above, down upon her.

Actual photograph of an Angel, Xitung, Egypt.

Suddenly, she smelled beautiful perfume of roses and gardenias. Moved by this elegant sense of peace and grace, she turned to her husband and whispered to him to "take a picture of the altar."

"What for?" he asked. "There's nobody there." She raised her voice emphatically and ordered him to, "Take the picture! Take the picture!" This documented photograph was the result and was produced from an original negative from their camera.

It is a verified photograph of an appearance of an angel. Many believe it is The Blessed Mother, Mary.

As you will notice, the man on the right side of the photograph is thrilled as he sees the angel. The man standing on the left is not looking toward the altar.

The candles at the altar are lit by those who have prayed to God. The physical candles in the lower central section are rising into the etheric octave to go to the heart of God. Thus, there are two levels and images of candles: one set in the physical, and one set rising into the spiritual octave of energy, the etheric, also known as the Heavenly realm, as the result of people who prayed to God who hears our prayers and always answers.

The bright, white rectangle in the upper right is a window in the back of the church behind the altar. The inscription over the altar canopy is Arabic for, "Peace to All who Enter Here."

The angel is wearing white garments with flowing robes of aqua, the Blessed Mother's traditional color often called, "Madonna Blue". In Ancient theology and modern apparitions or appearances of Mary, she is often in the identical aqua green.

It was reported that the negative was taken to Kodak's United States laboratory for examination. Kodak confirmed the photo was not a fake, that the images were actual and authentic, and they offered the gentleman and his wife a million dollars so Kodak could advertise "an actual photograph of an angel". In the 1980s, $1 million would have made this middle-class family rich.

But the family declined and declared this photograph belongs to prosperity to witness that angels are real and The Blessed Mother comes when we pray. We may not always see the angels, but we know they are with us if we believe and follow God's laws.

This is the true accounting of how this actual photograph of an appearance of The Blessed Mother, Mary, came to be.

Angel Blessings

May the Angels of God
Always Protect you.

May the Angels of God
Always Guide you.

May the Angels of God
Always Heal you, Caress you, and Love you.

May the Angels of God
Give you Hope, Peace, and Merciful Forgiveness.

May the Angels of God
Answer your every Prayer.

And,

May you be an Angel of God
and a Blessing to others.

God Bless You.

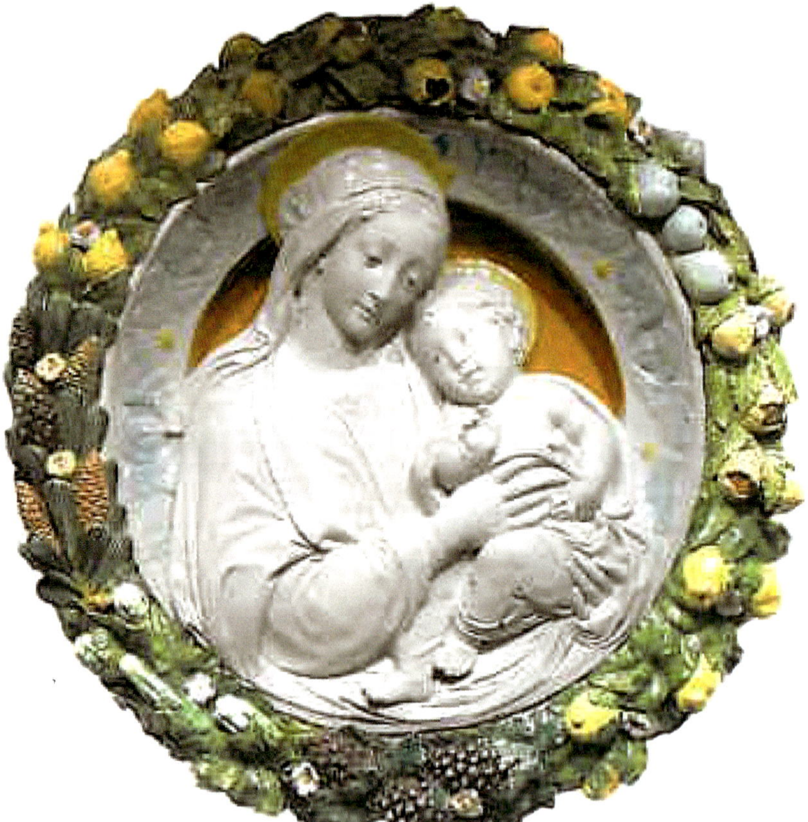

Best wishes,
A.C. Grone